# GETTING
# TO KNOW
# *the* GOSPEL
# OF
# *Matthew*

## Scott M. Lewis, sj

TWENTY
THIRD *23rd*
PUBLICATIONS
www.23rdpublications.com

**L**i**ving with Christ**
livingwithchrist.us

**Twenty-Third Publications**
1 Montauk Avenue, Suite 200, New London, CT 06320
(860) 437-3012 » (800) 321-0411 » www.23rdpublications.com

ISBN: 978-1-62785-047-6

Printed in Canada

# Contents

# Introduction

For centuries, the Gospel of Matthew was considered a 'church gospel' because of the abundance of teachings on prayer, community life, liturgy, and religious observance.

Early Church tradition associated this gospel with the figure of a man because it opens with the human genealogy of Jesus. (This figure reflects those depicted in Ezekiel 1:1-4 and 10:1-22.)

# Who was Matthew?

Matthew was probably written around 85 CE in one of the cities of Syria or Palestine. We do not know with certainty who the author was, although tradition associates him with Matthew the tax collector in Matthew 9:9. The same tax collector is called Levi son of Alphaeus in Mark 2:14 and Levi in Luke 5:27.

Matthew's community and his audience was thoroughly Jewish. Given the fierceness of his polemic against the Pharisees and the concern for hyper-observance of the Law and the continuing importance of Jewish customs, it is likely that this was a time of tension, competition, and separation. In targeting a Jewish audience, Mark made extensive use of the Old Testament prophetic texts for fulfillment quotations (1:22-23; 2:15, 17-18, 23; 4:14-16) in order to establish Jesus' credentials as the Messiah and to place him firmly within

Israel's salvation history. Matthew labored to portray his community as the true Israel and Jesus as the authoritative interpreter of the Law – a new Moses. The mission of Jesus was for the "lost sheep of the house of Israel" (10:5; 15:24) but at the end of the gospel, to "all nations" (28:19).

# Aspects Unique to Matthew

Uniquely in Matthew, Pontius Pilate washes his hands to demonstrate he is not guilty of the blood of Jesus. The crowd cries out, "His blood be on us and on our children!" (27:25). Written after the destruction of the Temple and the sack of Jerusalem, this reflects the belief that those events were divine retribution for the rejection and execution of Jesus. It was the source of the 'blood libel' against the Jewish people and the cause of much persecution at the hands of Christians. It is important to note that this is a consequence of the failure to understand the original context of this gospel and the pressures and events that influenced it. The collective guilt of the Jewish people was explicitly repudiated by Vatican II in the 1965 decree *Nostra Aetate* (In Our Age), which addressed the relation of the Church with non-Christian religions.

There is a long diatribe against the scribes and Pharisees in Mt 23:13-32 in which they are condemned and vilified. It is in Matthew that we find some of the most negative and strident comparisons of the teachings of Jesus with the practices of the Pharisees and other Jews. This contributed to making the word 'Pharisee' synonymous with hypocrisy, legalism, and obstinate refusal to believe. There is a strong possibility that these do not represent the actual words of Jesus but reflect what was going on in Matthew's time rather than the lifetime of Jesus. Undoubtedly Jesus was involved in controversies, but these harsh denunciations do not reflect the teachings and image of Jesus found elsewhere in this same gospel.

# The Kingdom of Heaven

The Kingdom of Heaven is one of the dominant themes in the Gospel of Matthew. Being a devout Jew, Matthew avoids direct reference to God and substitutes the more indirect and respectful Kingdom of 'Heaven'. The Kingdom of Heaven is mentioned extensively and refers to the dawning of the new age. A series of similes in 13:24-50 describe the hidden but powerful nature of the Kingdom of Heaven in terms of mustard seeds, leaven, hidden treasure, a pearl of great value, and weeds growing among the wheat.

Matthew is far more generous with honorific titles for Jesus than the other gospels. Jesus is called the Christ/Messiah, the Son of God, and the Son of David – a Messianic title. The term Emmanuel – 'God is with us' – was to be the name of Jesus in the angelic intervention in 1:23. Although he does not bear that name, there is an inference in 28:20, where the ascending Jesus assures his followers that he would be with them always until the end of the ages. The enigmatic self-reference used by Jesus – the Son of Man – is used numerous times. It refers to the humanity of Jesus, especially in relation to his suffering and death.

# Building on Mark

The Gospel of Mark is the main source for Matthew's gospel. Matthew reworks much of Mark to bring it into harmony with his own literary style and theological outlook. He refines Mark's Greek and omits or changes passages that seemed to put the disciples or the family of Jesus in a bad light. For example, he modifies Mark 9:10, where the disciples did not understand the resurrection from the dead. In Mark 10:35 the sons of Zebedee ask the favour of Jesus, while Matthew 20:20 places the request in the mouth of their mother. Matthew edits Jesus' reply to the rich young man in Mark 5:30-31 (Why do you call me good?) to read "Why do you ask me about what is good?" and Matthew 9:22 eliminates the impression that Jesus did not know who touched him (Mark 5:30-31).

# The New Moses

Matthew calls on a lot of material from a source that is common with the Gospel of Luke. The bulk of it is found in chapters 5-7, the Sermon on the Mount. There is a wealth of material that is Matthew's own, most of it in the Infancy Narrative in chapters 1 and 2 and the Passion narrative in 28:9-20 and 27:62-66. He also utilizes some special traditions about Peter, such as the account of his walking on water in 14:28-31 and his status as a result of his confession of Jesus in 16:17-19.

Chapters 1-2 comprise Matthew's Infancy Narrative, and it differs significantly from Luke's version. It is an expression of *Midrash*, which is Jewish biblical interpretation consisting of an imaginative retelling of a story or Scripture passage. Only in Matthew do we find the visit of the three Magi, the 'star' of Bethlehem, and the slaughter of the innocent children at the hands of Herod. The angels communicate only with Joseph through dreams. Mary does not speak in Matthew's story.

Jesus is portrayed in Matthew as the new Moses, and Herod as the mirror image of the wicked Pharaoh in Exodus, who ordered the deaths of newborn Hebrew males. The flight into Egypt is a similar miraculous escape of the deliverer. Many have doubted the historicity of the slaughter of the Holy Innocents because there is no record in any historical source such as Josephus. However, we know from those sources that Herod murdered one of his wives, a couple of his sons, and many 'enemies', so the story is very plausible.

Matthew's account of the baptism of Jesus basically follows Mark's but with some interesting additions. In Matt 3:13-17, we find a dialogue between John the Baptist and Jesus concerning the necessity of baptism for Jesus.

This answers the uneasy question that some early Christians asked – if John's baptism was one of repentance, what did it have to do with Jesus, the sinless one? In submitting to baptism, Jesus shows himself as the model of righteousness and obedience to God. The heavenly voice affirming the sonship of Jesus in 3:17 is very similar to Mark's account, but rather than being a private revelation directed at Jesus ('you'), it is public, to all Israel ('this' is my Son, the Beloved…').

Just as in Luke, Matthew's Jesus is tested in the desert by Satan. Jesus is a stand-in for Israel, who failed in their desert testing (Exodus and Numbers), complaining and rebelling against God. The test always begins with "If you are the Son of God…" and is geared to plant seeds of fear and mistrust of God in Jesus, thereby leading him to misuse his powers. Jesus has to affirm his absolute trust and his focus on the mission entrusted to him.

# The Beatitudes

In Matthew 5, Jesus begins his teaching to Israel as the new Moses in what we call the Sermon on the Mount or the Beatitudes. In 5:17, Jesus insists that he has not come to abolish the law or the prophets but to fulfill them. The Law was to remain in full force; in fact, Jesus raises the bar, insisting that his followers must outdo the scribes and Pharisees in righteousness. Matthew wrote as a Jew and in fact most of the Beatitudes and the subsequent teachings in chapters 5-7 can be found in the Jewish tradition.

He declares blessed by God those who are poor in spirit, those who mourn, the meek, those who hunger and thirst for righteousness, the merciful, pure in heart, peacemakers, and those who are persecuted for righteousness' sake. Everything will be theirs: solace, status as children of God, mercy, the inheritance of the land, righteousness, and the Kingdom of Heaven. The persecution they will receive should be a cause of rejoicing, for the prophets were persecuted in the same fashion. These teachings represent the tools of the kingdom, the conditions necessary for it to be present. Wherever they are practised, God's reign takes hold. These principles or teachings represent hope and are already present in the person of Jesus and his ministry. They define his life and he lives them out perfectly.

The community of followers is the salt of the earth and the light of the world – it functions as a sign of contradiction and hope to the world (5:13-16). Their deeds and righteousness are on behalf of the world.

"Blessed are the poor in spirit, for theirs is the kingdom of heaven" includes the economically poor, but Matthew expands the meaning so that it refers also to those who are devoid of arrogance and violence and humble before

God. They cling to God as their sole means of sustenance and support.

"Blessed are those who mourn, for they will be comforted" is a description of those who truly mourn for the fate and condition of the nation – Zion – and refuse to give in and accept it. They continually pray for the liberation and redemption of the nation. Those whose hearts are broken by the suffering and injustice they see and experience are truly those who mourn.

"Blessed are the meek, for they will inherit the earth" should not be understood as meek in our modern sense of the word. It is associated with humility, and can be described as kind, patient, and non-violent. It does not mean weakness or passivity.

"Blessed are those who hunger and thirst for righteousness, for they will be filled" is comfort and encouragement for those whose yearning for justice and righteousness before

God is as intense as human hunger and thirst. It assumes that this hunger and thirst will be directed towards action.

"Blessed are the merciful, for they will receive mercy" expresses the quality of God taken from the Old Testament – compassionate, merciful, and slow to anger. Note that in Matthew mercy is elevated over sacrifice (9:13 and 12:7); this is right from the Old Testament prophets.

"Blessed are the pure in heart, for they will see God" is an apt description of wanting, thinking, and feeling God's will and living that out in undivided obedience to God.

"Blessed are the peacemakers, for they will be called children of God" is an application of the unconditional and undivided love of all, including enemies, that Jesus commands in 5:44-48, as well as the emphasis on forgiveness in the Our Father, in 6:14-15.

"Blessed are those who are persecuted for righteousness' sake, for theirs is the kingdom of heaven. Blessed are you when people revile you and persecute you and utter all kinds of evil against you falsely on my account. Rejoice and be glad, for your reward is great in heaven, for in the same way they persecuted the prophets who were before you." Living the principles expressed in the Beatitudes will put one at odds with society and the world. This should be seen as a sign of being on the right path. According to the apocalyptic worldview, persecution and tribulations are a necessary part of birthing the new world.

# Living Life in the Kingdom

In the chapters that follow, Matthew's Jesus explains the 'how' of putting these principles into practice. In 5:21-26, he likens anger and insult to murder and insists on reconciliation before any worship of God takes place. The Jews believed in the power of speech for good or ill, hence the emphasis on blessings and curses. There are numerous examples in the Jewish tradition of stern prohibition of insulting speech or behavior – again, it was equated with the spilling of blood.

Keeping watch over external actions is not enough – 5:27-30 classifies even looking at a woman lustfully as adultery. What is acted on is first conceived in the mind and heart. Purity of mind is as important as purity of deed. Again, similar statements are numerous in the Jewish traditions at the time.

In Matthew, Jesus prohibits divorce twice – in 5:31-32 and 19:1-12. One account is adapted from Mark while the second is taken from the source Matthew shared with Luke. The attitude to divorce varied at the time. The Rabbi Hillel and his followers were more liberal in allowing divorce, while Rabbi Shammai took a much stricter position. Jesus aligns himself with the latter teacher.

With a strong emphasis on truthful speech in God's Kingdom, Jesus forbids the taking of oaths – using God's name falsely. Oath taking was widely criticized in antiquity in both pagan and Jewish sources.

# Some Challenging Sayings

Some of the most difficult sayings in the New Testament are found in 5:38-42. Followers of Jesus are not to resist an evildoer, but to turn the other cheek if struck. They are further urged to go the extra mile if pressed into service and to lend freely, expecting nothing in return. This is not an invitation to passivity or victimhood but to non-violent resistance. This breaks the cycle and spiral of violence that is based on revenge and wounded honor.

Jesus calls for a quality of love from his followers that imitates divine love. They are to love their enemies and pray for their persecutors. God makes no distinctions and sets no conditions for God's love – even the evil and ungrateful receive divine love and blessings. Enemies, Gentiles, persecutors, and others are to be loved – and that means practical concern and care, not necessarily personal preference. Biblical love is always practical and immediate, concerning itself with the needs of the other. The final exhortation is to "be perfect" as God is. The original Greek word means whole, complete, and undivided – in other words, love should be all-encompassing and not in any way divided or diminished. This is what it means to be a "child of the Most High God."

Judging others will only bring judgment on self (7:1-5) since people are blind to their own faults. The seeker who asks, seeks, and knocks will not be denied – the door to the kingdom will be opened and they will be rewarded for their persistent yearning (7:7-11). Deeds of spiritual power are not enough and they are not a sign of favour with God or personal sanctity. Repeating the name of the Lord, prophesying, casting out demons, and working miracles will earn no favour with Jesus – only those who take his teachings to heart and apply them will be transformed. In the parable of the fate of the two houses built on rock or sand, it is clear that believers were being prepared for life in the Kingdom of God and to be able to withstand the pressures of persecution and upheaval.

# The Golden Rule

Jesus repeats the Golden Rule – a form of it was used by almost every religion or philosophical system in antiquity. "In everything do to others as you would have them do to you; for this is the law and the prophets." The teachings come to an end with an insistence that the kingdom of God has a very narrow gate – the way to destruction is wide and the road easy. The road and gate that leads to life is hard and few find it. This is an example of the 'two-way' spirituality that is found in Deuteronomy, the Dead Sea Scrolls, and the Book of Wisdom.

The Our Father in 6:9-15 is a fervent eschatological prayer for God's reign to arrive soon. The one who prays addresses the prayer to the God who is above all and the God of all. There is the desire that God's name be hallowed – that is, that believers live their lives in a manner that elicits praise and glory for God. The divine will must be manifested on earth until earth becomes a mirror image of heaven. God must be depended on for daily sustenance and strength. Debts – sins – will be forgiven only to the extent that we have forgiven others. There is a fervent wish not to be put to the test, but if that occurs, to be delivered. The entire prayer reflects oneness, forgiveness, the rule of God, God's glorification, and perseverance in the face of trials.

# The Final Judgment

The final judgment scene in 25:31-46 is probably one of the most vivid and well-known scenes in the New Testament. At the judgment, the people will be gathered before the Son of Man to be separated like sheep and goats. Those admitted to the kingdom will be told by Jesus that they gave him food when he was hungry, drink when he was thirsty, welcome when he was a stranger, clothes when he was naked, care when he was sick, and visitation when he was in prison. When they ask in puzzlement when they did such things, he will reply, "just as you did it to one of the least of these who are members of my family, you did it to me." In a negative form of this exchange, those who failed to do these things for him – and to the least – will be rejected and cast into eternal fire. None of the praiseworthy deeds is explicitly religious in nature, but consists in an active, compassionate response to those in need.

For Matthew, forgiveness is a sign of God's Kingdom and a prerequisite for entrance. At the end of the Our Father in 6:14-15, Matthew reiterates the prayer's insistence on forgiveness with his insistence that those who refuse to forgive others cannot expect God to forgive them their sins. This point is hammered home in 18:21-22 with Jesus' insistence that one should forgive another "seventy times seven" times – in other words, limitlessly. This is followed by the Parable of the Unforgiving Debtor in 18:23-35 that in dramatic form illustrates the absolute necessity of forgiveness.

As in Mark and Luke, Matthew relates the confession of Peter on the way to Caesarea Philippi (16:13-20). In Matthew's version, however, Peter is signaled out for exception praise from Jesus. He is given his new name – 'rock' – and the status of foundation of the community, along with authority and the keys of the kingdom. Peter was probably associated with Matthew's community and was their living link with the historical Jesus.

Matthew follows Mark's account of the Last Supper, arrest, and crucifixion very closely but with a few additions unique to Matthew. At the institution of the Eucharist, the blood of the covenant will be poured out for the forgiveness of sins. Judas' remorse and suicide is described in 27:3-10, and in 27:19 Pilate's wife warns him to not get involved with Jesus because of her disturbing dream.

In the narration of the crucifixion, the death of Jesus is accompanied by earthquakes, the splitting of rocks, and the opening of tombs (27:51-53). Many of the dead saints are seen in the city. This highlights the apocalyptic 'end-time' nature of the death of Jesus and the beginning of the final days. In the resurrection scene (28:2-4), a dazzling angel descends to the tomb and rolls aside the stone rather than the tomb already being open.

Matthew 27:62-66 and 28:11-15 are Matthew's additions for the purpose of counteracting Jewish claims that the disciples of Jesus had stolen his body during the night. With the guard posted this would have been impossible, but as the text states, that was the story circulating among the Jews even at the time the gospel was written.

# The Great Commission

The eleven disciples meet Jesus on the designated mountain in Galilee. Even then, some continue to doubt. Jesus assures them that all authority in heaven and on earth has been given to him. In what is called the 'great commission' he commands them to go and make disciples of all nations and share everything that Jesus had taught them – the movement now has a universal mission. They are to also baptize in the name of the Father, the Son, and the Holy Spirit. The gospel ends with a reassurance and promise from Jesus to them and to those who follow him today: "Remember, I am with you always, to the end of the age.' Jesus is truly Emmanuel – God with us.

**Rev. Scott Lewis, S.J.,** is Dean of Regis College, the Jesuit Faculty in the Toronto School of Theology at the University of Toronto, where he is an associate professor of New Testament studies. He has worked and taught in Jerusalem, served as Director of Manresa Jesuit Spiritual Renewal Centre in Pickering, Ontario, and has a regular column on Scripture in *The Catholic Register.*